MW00595550

the
REAL HEAVEN

it's not what you think

the
REAL HEAVEN
it's not what you think

JOE BEAM
LEE WILSON

COVENANT

www.covenantpublishing.com

P.O. Box 390 Webb City, Missouri 64870
Call toll free at 877.673.1015

Library of Congress Cataloging-in-Publication Data
Beam, Joe.
The real heaven : it's not what you think / Joe Beam, Lee Wilson.
    p. cm.
ISBN 1-892435-53-5 (alk. paper)
1. Heaven—Christianity. 2. Heaven—Biblical teaching. I. Wilson, Lee, 1980- II. Title.
BT846.3.B43 2006
236'.25—dc22

                          2006009109

Cover design by Ken Fox.
Book design by Mandie Tepe.

CONTENTS

IN LOVING MEMORY OF...

JIMMY ALLEN

DARLENE BARNETT

JOHN R. BEAM

LUCIEN & LOIS HILYER

CHARLES JOHNSON

GROVER & MARY JOHNSON

HOUSTON (HOOT) JONES

BENNIE LEE & OMIE MCGEE

BILLY MCGEE

WILL PANEL

LAMAR & CHLOE PLUNKETT

ARLAND STAMPS

CLAYBURN STAMPS

GEORGE & MATTIE STAMPS

MARIE STAMPS

RAYMOND & MARY NELL STAMPS

JAMES LEE & DESSIE WILSON

BO, BULLET, REBEL, ROCKY, AND YODA

LEE WOULD LIKE TO THANK...

Special thanks to my wife Joanna and our sons, Jacob and Tyler for their patience during the writing of this book when "family time" often happened while I was in another room pecking on my computer. I love you all more than life itself. Joanna, you make Heaven a place on earth.

Thanks to my dad and mom for their love, support and raising me in a home where the Bible was the text book for life. If not for them, I likely would not ever see Heaven. I love you more than words can say.

Thanks to my brother, Josh, for his service to the world as a solider in the United States Navy. If not for his selflessness, and the service of others like him such as my dad and grandpa, I might not have the freedom to express my opinions in a book such as this. Thank you!

Thanks to my grandmothers, Marie Stamps and Empress Wilson for being powerful examples of Jesus Christ. Thanks to my grandfathers, Laymond Stamps and Paul Wilson for showing me that the best sermon is a life of integrity, courage and smiles while walking humbly with God.

Thanks to my in-laws, Joe, Alice, Angel and Kimberly. Being family with you is beyond simply "law." Thank you for making me a real part of your family. I love you. Additionally, thank you, Joe, for inviting me to be part of this book. It is an honor to write with my favorite writer.

Thanks to Steve Cable, my main editor at Covenant Publishing, for his encouragement, suggestions and verbal fist pumps despite the fact that his knee bent in different directions (literally) during this project.

JOE WOULD LIKE TO THANK...

Alice, Angel, Joanna and Kimberly for their loving commitment and continuing support.

The staff at Family Dynamics Institute for working to change the world through strengthening marriages and families.

Lee Wilson for his dedication to this project.

INTRODUCTION

by JOE BEAM

AN EXPLANATION OF HOW DREAD TURNED TO HOPE

For years, I thought I was the only one. I kept it quiet, like some nasty secret that will haunt and humiliate you if others find out. I even wondered if it might be heresy, that maybe God Himself was thoroughly disgusted with me. One thing was for sure, if He had written me off because of this, then I wouldn't have to be afraid any longer because it wasn't going to happen.

You see, I was terrified by the entire concept of Heaven.

I'd read enough, heard enough sermons, and even preached some of my own about the terrors of Hell, so I was absolutely convinced I wanted nothing to do with that tortuous place. But to me, the opposite choice was almost as scary. Living in a place for eternity, singing or worshipping or whatever they do up there with no endings, transitions or changes? I couldn't see how anyone wanted to be in a prison like that, especially one that was never, ever going to end. I felt trapped; it was either that or Hell, and I wanted neither of them.

There were days when the idea of complete annihilation appealed to me more.

Once I tried talking to another minister about it. I hoped he would give me some insight that would clear my mind, heal my fear, and give me a peace about the afterlife I had given to so many others when death came knocking.

Oh, I knew the right words to say to a dying person, as well as his family, and spoke them convincingly. I actually believed them. They gave comfort to the people to whom I ministered, but they just made my own fears worse.

So, over coffee, with no little amount of emotion, I poured my trepidation out on the table and waited for him to set me straight and end my apprehension. His reply? "Well, personally, I really look forward to heaven." And that was that. He never mentioned it again.

The only other time I gave it a try was with a man who is a true shepherd in the kingdom of God. He has helped so many people in so many ways that I decided to risk it once again. I summoned enough courage to tell him about my fear. He replied, "I feel the same way. Dying and going to Heaven forever scares me beyond my ability to explain. I've tried to figure it out and think that maybe it's the idea of having no control over my life or choices or anything else. I don't want to live like a robot."

I listened carefully, wondering if that's what drove my fears, but found nothing in his words that gave me any understanding of myself and nothing that gave me any decrease in emotional turmoil. Maybe there was some small comfort in finding a fellow sufferer, but there wasn't even a hint of a cure.

I never shared my own fears again, at least not that I can remember, but I began to listen carefully as others talked about Heaven. To my surprise, I wasn't the only one who wasn't excited about going there. More and more, I heard Christians who loved God and lived godly lives mention their fear of eternity in Heaven. One brother said, "You people who like to sing will enjoy it there. I don't get into worship like you do and can't imagine I'll be happy doing that for eternity." Others made statements that were nearly as bold as the emotions I felt.

Don't think that I spent inordinate amounts of time thinking about death and the life beyond. It hardly ever came to mind. It's just that when it did, I felt this churning in the pit of my stomach and almost a panic that every day I was closer to facing this than I had ever been before. Maybe a couple times a year it would come sneaking into my thoughts. I'd be depressed for a couple hours and then not think of it again for months on end. It wasn't like I was obsessed; most of the time it just didn't exist for me.

There were things about Heaven that really attracted me. I could even talk about Heaven in terms of my loved ones who'd gone on and feel happy for them. I would sometimes think of how Heaven is going to be a totally different existence for my mentally handicapped daughter, Angel. She won't be "different" there. I looked forward to having conversations with her there that I can never have here because of her lack of understanding.

It's just the idea of living there forever that made my blood run cold.

Dr. Jerry Rushford was kind enough to invite me to speak at the

Annual Bible Lectures at Pepperdine University in Malibu, California. When he asked me my topic of choice, I decided to speak on the afterlife. Of the three lectures assigned, I spoke once on where the dead are, once on what Hell is like, and once on what Heaven is like.

I presented those lectures in May of 2004. My only regret is that I hadn't prepared for and delivered them a long time before. As I researched, studied, and meditated, I learned that my concept of Heaven was far from the mark. It will last forever; that part is true. However, it isn't just standing around singing forever and ever and ever. Nor is it a life that is so unlike this that we have no way to relate or anticipate its joys.

Heaven is a new life. A better life to be sure, but a life that is in many ways like the life we live here. It has relationships, variety, excitement, and emotional fulfillment. We won't be regimented robots but will have the ability to think, choose and act.

That's what we want to show you in this book. My son-in-law, Lee Wilson, co-authored this book with me. He brings a unique perspective on the Word and life, and his involvement makes this a better book than it would have been otherwise.

Are you ready for an adventure? Ready to have your thoughts on Heaven challenged, maybe even changed? Ready to get excited about the place that awaits those who love God?

Well, for the first time in my life, I am excited! By the time you finish this study, I think you might be, too.

HEAVEN IS AN ACTUAL PLACE

"Heaven is a state of mind!" he yelled to his audience. "You're situation will never be perfect, so you must learn to choose happiness and contentment!"

Perhaps you have heard self-help gurus use similar words to encourage positive thinking. It sounds familiar, doesn't it?

In Philippians 4:11, Paul says, *"I have learned to be content whatever the circumstances."*

Certainly, we should strive to follow Paul's example by choosing contentment even when our situation is not ideal. But, does that mean we dismiss the concept of one day living a completely fulfilling existence that makes us happy without any mental compensations? If we accept the Bible's teachings about Heaven, we don't have to abandon that idea. In fact, the Bible tells us to look forward to that world of total happiness and fulfillment when we are feeling sad or depressed.

The Bible tells us Heaven is as real as your own backyard. That means that when we are there, no one will have to convince us that we are truly experiencing Heaven. We will not have to "open our minds" or "listen with our hearts" to experience it; we will know it is absolute reality.

Heaven will not be some vaporous, transparent illusion, but it will be a real place that can be seen, smelled, touched, heard and tasted.

Based on the teachings of the Bible, we know God will destroy the current earth and universe because of sin's contamination. The Bible also tells us that God will replace them with something much better—new heavens and a New Earth (2 Peter 3:13). In fact, the new heavens and earth will so overshadow the old that Isaiah 65:17 tells us the old will not even "come to mind."

What is real to us now will no longer exist, but something that is *just as real* will replace what we know. We will not exist in a place that is short of being the "real world," but rather we will exist in a replacement world that will last forever.

HEAVEN IS NOT JUST A FUTURE CONCEPT

When the Bible uses the word *Heaven* or *heavens*, sometimes it is talking about the sky; other times, the universe; and still other times, the Heaven where God reigns on this throne. As you probably expected, this book is not about the sky or the universe, but the Heaven where God dwells and reigns on His throne.

The Bible tells us that beings traveled to and from Heaven, including Jesus, who said in John 6:33 that He came from Heaven to earth to give life to the world. In addition to Jesus coming to earth from Heaven, the Bible says angels, God's Holy Spirit, and humans traveled between the two. (John 1:32, Acts 1:2, 2 Corinthians 12:2, Revelation 10:1).

Therefore, according to the Bible, Heaven will not only be real to us in the future, but it has been a place of activity and consciousness in the past.

I have always taken hope from Jesus's words in John 14:2 that say He will "prepare a place" in Heaven for people who follow Him. When Jesus appeared on earth in His resurrected body, He told His followers He had to return to the Father in order to prepare a special place for us.

Though we might think of Jesus's work as being finished when He left the earth, it seems that it had only just begun. Jesus made us suitable for Heaven by giving Himself on the cross, but His next project was to make *Heaven* suitable for us. Not only did Jesus come to earth to alter the course of history, He returned to Heaven to lead a revolution there as well so that we could live with Him. So think of Jesus's alterations of Heaven as "Heaven: Part 2—Humans Now Welcome."

We often think that Jesus humbled Himself by working as a carpenter while in His human body, but I cannot imagine a more appropriate job for the creator of the earth and stars than carpentry. It is possible that Jesus chose that line of work because of His passion for building and improving. He would have been able to use His ability to design and create to build a bed that would provide rest for someone at the end of a long day; a house to shield the rain and provide a family with a lifetime of memories; or a boat to see the ends of the earth or to provide for a fishermen's family. How could the God we know resist doing what He loves to do and can do better than any being in existence? God is such a passionate creator and builder that He continued to do so while on earth.

So it's not that the concept of Heaven is too good to be true. It's that my limited mind could never harness enough imagination to paint an accurate picture of the work that the Master Creator has *yet* to finish. If He created this world and universe in only seven days, how could anyone possibly fathom what He could do with over 2000 years in which to work?

That does not mean God left us in the dark concerning Heaven and the afterlife. We certainly don't know all of His plans, but we have more to go on than mere speculation and guesswork. God provides previews of Heaven in the Bible that can give us hope and anticipation to help us persevere when this life is difficult.

Perhaps as you read this book, your God-given imagination will allow you a glimpse into the world of eternity with the King of creativity.

WHAT WILL WE BE IN HEAVEN?

"Heaven will be vastly different from this life."

I'm sure you have heard that said hundreds or even thousands of times. At different times in my life, I've imagined my existence in Heaven as being anything from universal exploration to a secluded trap in which I am absent of free will or a single independent thought.

One of the reasons my imagination often entertains scenarios of the new world I will one day experience is because I have only experienced this world; it is natural for me to imagine others. But what fuels my curiosity as much as the phenomenon of Heaven is the future condition of something with which I am very familiar— me. What will I be like in Heaven? Will I still have my memories, emotions, and personality? Will I still have those unique qualities that make me, *me?* Or will Heaven strip me entirely of my personal identity and idiosyncrasies?

WHAT ARE HUMANS?

To determine if humans will be different in the afterlife, we must first understand what it means to be human.

We are a unique bunch. Based on what the Bible tells us, humans were the last beings God created. I don't just mean that God created us after He made the animals on earth. I mean that God created us even after He created heavenly beings (angels). We were created to have a different role and place in the universe than any other creature.

If you have read any of my other books, you may recall a consistent theme of discussion on what I refer to as the triune nature of humans, that we consist of three inseparable components. We are *body*, meaning we are physical bodies of flesh and blood (Hebrews 2:14); we are *mind*, meaning we are both intellectual and emotional (Mark 5:15); and we are *spirit*, meaning there is a part of us that was formed within us by God Himself (Zechariah 12:1, Ecclesiastes 12:7).

A human is not human without all of those parts. I'm not me without my body, my mind and my spirit all together at the same time. That is what makes me human. You see, God and the angels are essentially spirits, though they are capable of inhabiting human bodies and even animals according to the Bible (John 4:24, Hebrews 1:14). Consider a few examples:

- Angels appeared as men to Abraham and Lot (Genesis 18-19).

- Angels can appear as horses or chariots of fire (2 Kings 2:11; 6:17).

- An angel who looked like a "young man" told Mary Magdalene, Mary the mother of Jesus, and Salome that Jesus had risen from the dead (Mark 16:5-7).

- In Hebrews 13:2, the point is made, "Do not forget to entertain strangers, for by doing so, some people have entertained angels without knowing it." (For further study on angels and spiritual beings, see "Seeing the Unseen")

What makes humans different from God and the angels is that we are spiritual *and* physical. It's not that we are spirits who happen to inhabit a body or a body waiting for a spirit, but by our very nature, we are both spirit and body. That is what makes us unique as human beings—we are not fully human without both.

Therefore, here is a very important question for us to consider concerning our existence in Heaven: "Will we still be human?"

When God raises us from the dead, will we become something other than human? Will we become another species? A different life form entirely?

start with RESURRECTION BODIES

The Bible provides eyewitness accounts as to what we will be like when God raises us from the dead. When Jesus died, God raised Him from the dead with a new kind of body, and, when He ascended into Heaven, He remained in that body. Do you remember some

21

of the things Jesus did in His "resurrection body?"

John 21 says Jesus walked, talked and even ate food while in His "new" body. Those activities are very human and entirely physical.

Further evidence that He was in an actual body and not a disembodied spirit comes from Jesus Himself when He said to His disciples, "A ghost does not have flesh and bones, *as you see I have*" (Luke 24:37-39). Flesh? Bones? His body had all the ingredients of being some kind of a human one.

Jesus even told Thomas to touch Him so that all could see He was physically real. Since He was not a "ghost" or a bodiless spirit, it makes sense to me that He was in some kind of an improved human body.

When our loved ones die -- we cannot see them. Jesus still had work to do

Several other passages (1 Corinthians 15:20, 48-49; Phil. 3:21; 1 John 3:2) tell us that the resurrected body of Jesus was a prototype or beta version of the bodies we will have. Philippians 3:21 calls it a "glorious body" and says that our bodies will be made "like His."

> *"But Christ has indeed been raised from the dead, the first fruits of those who have fallen asleep. For since death came through a human being, the resurrection of the dead comes also through a human being"* (1 Corinthians 15:20).

Jesus was the first to experience the "resurrection of the dead." He is the second Adam in that He is the first "new" kind of human. That means that we as God's children, like Jesus, will receive new bodies that are capable of entering Heaven.

OUR CURRENT BODIES

In 1 Corinthians 15 Paul calls our current bodies "seeds" for our resurrection bodies and suggests that God will use our current bodies to form our resurrection bodies, just as a farmer uses a seed to grow a plant. Obviously, we would not expect a carrot seed to grow corn nor would we expect a human seed to grow another species or creature.

Paul goes on to say that the seed of our current bodies will be "sown a perishable body [but] it is raised an imperishable body. It is sown in dishonor; it is raised in glory. It is sown in weakness; it is raised in power. It is sown a natural body; it is raised a spiritual body. If there is a natural body, there is also a spiritual body." (1 Corinthians 15:42-44).

Notice that Paul says "a spiritual body." He does not say a bodiless spirit. By having a body and a spirit, we will keep the qualities that make us human when we are resurrected. But without sin having power over our bodies, our spirits will be in intimate fellowship with God and will lead our bodies (rather than our bodies leading our spirits, as is often the case in this life).

CAN A RESURRECTION BODY REMEMBER THE FORMER LIFE?

While in that spirit-led body, the body the Bible tells us is like the body we will receive, Jesus remembered what had happened before He died. He maintained His memories and knowledge, including His friends, His mission, and directions to the meeting

23

place of His disciples. He was still Himself, though in an improved body. He had not lost His identity, and other humans could still recognize Him, though there was something visually different about His new body because they did not recognize Him right away. It could have been that Jesus chose to disguise Himself or that His body looked slightly different and even close friends needed a few minutes before they could recognize Him.

We can safely assume Jesus still had a body that appeared Jewish in race because other Jews freely spoke with Him. That would have been very unusual if He looked non-Jewish in that day because the Jews were not to associate with other tribes and cultures.

Passages such as Revelation 7:9 imply that our own bodies will maintain certain racial traits in the resurrected form.

"After this I looked, and there before me was a great multitude that no one could count, from every nation, tribe, people and language, standing before the throne and in front of the Lamb."

Because God fashioned a culturally diverse humanity, it makes sense for Him to restore a diverse humanity in Heaven.

WILL WE RECOGNIZE EACH OTHER?

The idea that we will recognize each other in the afterlife as the disciples recognized Jesus is consistently supported in Scripture. In the parable of the rich man and Lazarus, Jesus portrayed both men recognizing each other, despite the fact that one lived in paradise and the other in torment.

Matthew 17:1-4 reports that Moses and Elijah appeared to Jesus and discussed His mission with Him. The disciples recognized Moses and Elijah, even though Jesus had not revealed their identities, and the disciples couldn't have previously known what Moses and Elijah looked like because photography and portraits did not yet exist. This seems to suggest that we will be able to recognize people in the afterlife whom we have not even met but know by reputation alone.

Perhaps we will be able to recognize others by their reputation because our new bodies will somehow allow individual personality to illuminate through.

In Luke 24, Jesus shows the disciples the nail scars in His hands. Somehow His scars remained, even though God brought Him back to life and gave Him a new body. Perhaps His scars were actually something coming from His spirit and were tools to help others recognize Him, a mark or a branding of sorts so that all would know His identity just by looking.

What if the scars were there as symbols of His love, an honor lifting Him up forever as the pinnacle of love that He will always be?

Perhaps our new bodies will also have traits by which others will recognize us. Scars, wrinkles and other things that may seem undesirable to us now will have different values and meanings in

Heaven. Remember, the Bible tells us that we see "but a poor reflection as in a mirror" (1 Cor. 13:12). In other words, we don't see the whole truth in this current existence. The beauty of the scars on the hands of Jesus was not the scars themselves; it was the love Jesus had for us that propelled Him into sacrificing Himself.

In Heaven, we will see the scars of those who were martyred as beautiful, rather than hideous. Such markings won't be imperfections in the body but rather a spiritual symbol of glory and honor. However, I am certainly not saying that those who are deformed or have health problems will take those burdens to Heaven with them.

One of the signs that foretold the coming of the kingdom of Heaven was healing. Heaven is healing of the mind, body and spirit. Disabilities and deformities will not exist in Heaven, though I believe that some signs of honor for sufferings in this life will be evident.

We may not be able to know exactly how, but we can know that the Bible supports the idea that we will *somehow* be able to recognize each other in Heaven. We will know our family members, friends and perhaps even some people we thought of as enemies.

The descriptions of grand reunions with family and loved ones who died before us are very true, and don't let anyone tell you otherwise!

Our new bodies will maintain our memories, emotions and impressions of this world. I'm often stunned when people speculate that we will have no memories of this first life in the next. In their minds, God will remove our memories and leave us in an eternal zombie-like state in which we are forbidden from independent thought or remembering where we came from.

Only a "god" who is completely out of touch with humanity would plan a "Heaven" like that. The Bible tells us we are to store up for ourselves, *"treasures in heaven, where neither moth nor rust consumes and where thieves do not break in and steal"* (Matthew 6:20 NRSV). Yet some would believe that God Himself becomes the thief by stealing our very memories and thoughts.

God is not out of touch and is not afraid of the truth. He has no desire of holding a tyrannical control over His people by forbidding memories, emotions and ideas. In fact, God created humans to remember, feel and think. It was His idea to begin with and when God created Adam and Eve with human traits, He called His creation "good." God will restore, not remove, what is good.

Your memories will not be stolen, erased or deleted. God loves us just the way He created us and with Him in charge, it's okay to be a human being. You will be loved and accepted as the person that has been molded in part by your experiences. You will remember this first life and the lessons learned from it and will be all the more grateful for the return to what God called "good."

SUPERNATURAL ABILITIES OF THE RESURRECTION BODY

Not only was the "beta-version" resurrection body of Jesus physical, but it also had the ability to overcome some physical laws. His body could walk through locked doors, as He did to enter the room where His disciples were meeting (John 20:19), and disappear into thin air, as He did at Emmaus (Luke 24:31). Though His body was physical, it could operate above the abilities of our current physical bodies. Its ability was supernatural and apparently powered by a supercharged spirit capable of direct fellowship with God. It could be that Jesus had the ability to overcome the laws of nature simply because He was God. Our resurrection bodies might not have those abilities. But the high-powered body we will receive will no longer be suppressed by sin's curse and will therefore be able to perform at its peak.

Human bodies in the Garden of Eden were superior to our current ones as well. Not only did those physical bodies live forever, but they never even got sick. Because of the emergence of sin, both of those strengths were lost. It seems to follow that when sin is removed, as it will be in Heaven, that humans will once again have physical and spiritual abilities far above current levels.

WHAT AGE WILL OUR NEW BODIES BE?

As far as we know, God created Adam and Eve as fully-grown, fully-developed humans. They were adults at their full potential and the finished human product. For adult humans to reproduce, very small humans are conceived, birthed and over several years develop into full-grown humans. At the present, aging beyond full-grown is deterioration and anything before full-grown, though still fully human, is not completely developed. But a human in paradise exists in a fully developed body that is at its full potential. Our bodies will remain at full potential without any negative affects of aging because God provides access to the Tree and the River of Life in Heaven (Revelation 21:6; 22:1-3, 14, 19). If you recall, God removed the Tree of Life after Adam and Eve sinned. Without access to that tree, human bodies can't stand the test of time. When God restores what is good, He will restore our rights to eat the food from His tree and our bodies will have ceaseless life.

WILL WE BECOME ANGELS?

When Tweety Bird finally killed his arch nemesis Tom Cat, Tom flew with his new angel wings to a cloud and sat down to strum a harp.

Clarence Oddbody worked diligently as George Bailey's guardian angel in the classic Christmas movie, "It's a Wonderful Life." You may remember that Clarence used to be a human being but temporarily left Heaven to "earn his wings" by showing George what life would have been like if he never existed.

Many other cartoons and movies portray people becoming angels when they die. I'm sure that neither the Tweety Bird cartoon nor the movie "It's a Wonderful Life" wanted to make theological statements; however, the entertainment industry has contributed to the common misconception that we cease to be humans after death and instead become angels.

Hebrews 2:14-26 explains that humans and angels are two totally different types of beings. Angels existed before God created humans; so it stands to reason God wasn't trying to make more angels when He created us. He originally intended for human beings to exist in the Garden of Eden, like Adam and Eve did before the fall. Sin put us out of the garden and out of the kind of fellowship Adam and Eve originally had with God.

God never tells us that we will become angels. Some might point to Matthew 22:30 as evidence that we will be angels, but read this passage closely:

> *"At the resurrection people will neither marry nor be given in marriage; they will be like the angels in Heaven."*

How will we be like the angels in Heaven? Only in that we will not "marry or be given in marriage." The comparison is limited to the ability to "marry or be given in marriage."

When we die, God uses our former bodies as seed and makes us better humans—not nonhumans.

ARE WE TRAPPED SPIRITS?

Another idea we're often taught is that the real us is currently trapped by our physical bodies, and we are really just spirits waiting to escape our humanity. Gilbert Ryle, author of *The Concept of the Mind* calls this the "ghost in a machine" theory. Many songs that are popular to Christians today often talk of tearing away our bodies to reveal the "real us." That idea may sound poetic and righteous, but that does not make it true.

In fact, Paul dealt with that false teaching in his day. The Gnostics in the day of the early church believed that a great separation existed between the physical and the spiritual and claimed that anything physical was entirely evil, while anything spiritual was entirely good.

That flawed belief system led the Gnostics to several erroneous conclusions. One of those conclusions was that God could not have created humans or the earth and universe because He was absolutely separate from anything physical.

Another teaching of Gnosticism claimed that Jesus didn't really come to earth in the flesh but was a spirit or ghost. Since Gnostics considered the physical entirely evil they didn't believe that a perfect person could live in a physical body or be born of a physical, human woman.

Furthermore, Gnosticism held the belief that our physical bodies and our spirits were not connected at all and, because of that, Gnostics believed people were free to let their bodies follow any physical passion or commit any sin without actually sinning because they believed the spirit could not sin.

Yet it was sin that caused God to cast Satan and the angels who followed him out of Heaven (2 Peter 2:4, Jude 1:6, Revelation 12:7-9, Ezekiel 28:12-18). Because the Bible tells us that angels, who are entirely spiritual beings, sinned, we can see that physical bodies are not alone in their ability to sin despite the claims of Gnosticism.

The teachings of Gnosticism are similar to the belief systems of Buddhism and Hinduism in that the focus is on escaping the physical body to find the imprisoned inner self that exists without the body. Biblical Christianity defies this notion and refuses to give up on humanity as God created it.

Our trouble is not that our bodies are entirely evil and entrap our entirely righteous spirits; it is that we have sinned spiritually *and* physically. Our spirits rebel against God by using our bodies for unholy things. The sinful nature of man causes our bodies to have passions and desires that are not righteous. Because our spirits are also affected by the sinful nature, the spiritual part of us acts as an accomplice at times, while at other times acts as the mastermind behind a sin. When Satan's armies of tempters are considered in the equation, you can see how one side of us might even be pitted against the other.

Because we were *not* created with a sinful nature but contracted it, we are out of balance with our original selves, and thus, our bodies and spirits are unable to achieve the level of unity that God intended.

When we allow God's Holy Spirit to unite with our own, we are able to again connect body and spirit to do what is righteous.

Before what is commonly known as "the Fall," the human body and spirit were one. The spirit used the body for purposes of the spirit and the body and spirit were united in purpose and mission. Now, there is a separation in which the body and spirit are often traveling in different directions. Not so in the new world where our spirits and bodies will reunite as God intended. You see, it is not that humans in their created, natural state are mistakes or inherently evil. It is that we are not in our natural state. Unlike the teachings of ancient Gnostics who taught that the only way to our true selves was to expel our bodies, we will reunite, not only with God, but *with ourselves*. We will no longer look into the mirror and lament at how unpredictable and disappointing we are. In Heaven, we will finally get to know the real us that God created—body, mind and spirit.

WILL BABIES AND SMALL CHILDREN BE IN HEAVEN?

A concern of parents who have lost babies or small children to death is what happens to them after they die. Because their children were not old enough to accept God's gift of salvation, parents sometimes wonder if God will receive their children into Heaven.

In Matthew 19:14, Jesus says, *"Let the little children come to me, and do not forbid them; for of such is the kingdom of heaven"* (NKJV).

Jesus was speaking of the childlikeness of faith and teaching that true believers come to God with an attitude much like that of a small child—completely dependent, without any strengths or resources of their own, and with a natural, doubtless trust. Jesus further said to adults, *"Unless you change and become as little children, you will never enter the kingdom of heaven"* (Matthew 18:3).

Matthew 19:14 should bring hope to parents who have had miscarriages and lost young children. By comparing believers to small children, Jesus showed us that God has a tender heart toward little ones who must be dependant on others. With no works of their own in which to boast and no strength to be self-reliant, they'll have nothing but God's mercy when they stand before Him. I can't imagine that the same Savior who said "of such is the kingdom of heaven," concerning children would forbid them from entering.

In Deuteronomy 1:39 Moses told Israel that he would not be allowed to enter the Promised Land because of his actions against God. However, Moses said God *would* allow innocent children who didn't know right from wrong, to enter the Promised Land. So it seems clear that God provides a special grace to those who *"have no knowledge of good and evil"* as Deuteronomy 1:39 suggests.

The punishment of Hell is reserved for people who have willingly and knowingly sinned against God (Romans 1:29-31; Galatians 5:19-21; Revelations 21:8). Hell is not for innocent children. Though we live in a sinful, fallen world that is punished because of the sin of Adam, salvation is determined individually. God does not place guilt on children for the sins of their ancestors or anyone else for that matter. In fact, Ezekiel 18:20 says, *"The one who sins is the one who will die. The child will not share the guilt of the parent, nor will the parent share the guilt of the child."*

Babies and children who pass from this life will go safely to the arms of God. Perhaps their bodies will grow to full potential while they are awaiting the rest of humanity to join them. Or maybe they automatically reach full potential the moment they enter paradise. The bottom line is that babies, small children and the mentally handicapped are not held responsible for their actions by God because they are without the mental capacities to knowingly rebel against Him. God receives them into Heaven and will take very good care of them until they are reunited with their families.

CHAPTER 3

WHAT HAPPENS WHEN HUMANS DIE?

At times I've thought of death as relief from the anxiety of not knowing what lies beyond my current life. At other times, I've dreaded death to the point that I've struggled to function.

I vividly remember a summer day from my childhood when I was probably seven or eight years old. The Alabama sun blazed down as my mother and grandmother walked outside with me, enjoying the blue skies. As my grandmother sat on a bench and watched me play, I took note of her in comparison to my mother. The sun seemed to affect her much more than my mother, and the lines on her face were much more noticeable as her makeup ran with her sweat.

To protect me from my terror of death even before that day, my parents would sometimes avoid driving by graveyards. I just could not grip the fact that one day my body would stop working and I would die.

As I panicked at the remembrance of this terrifying issue, I approached my mother and grandmother and told them my fears had returned. My grandmother took me in her arms, and she and my mother tried to encourage me by telling me about how wonderful

Heaven would be. At that young age, I could not imagine anything being better than my current life, and I was angry at the thought of God taking away anyone I loved.

Talking to me about Heaven did not alleviate my breakdown, and so my grandmother began tossing me in the air a few inches and catching me. She jokingly said that my fears would be gone when I fell back into her arms.

My fears didn't go anywhere.

As life went on, I learned to adjust to the fear of death in some ways; mostly I ignored the issue altogether, going out of my way to avoid it.

Several years after that incident, I behaved terribly at my other grandmother's funeral by joking around and playing games in an attempt to shield myself from a subject that refused to grant me relief.

I understand now why I acted the way I did and imagine that many children and adults struggle with the concept of death. Perhaps that struggle will not be completely gone until we join God in Heaven, but I'm convinced that much of the fear and dread of death can be overcome through the power of God's Word and His Holy Spirit. It seems that many of the teachings of today concerning death and the afterlife are simply not based on biblical teachings. That's partly why so many are not excited about Heaven. The message of the Bible concerning these things is much more assuring than the message of the day.

WHAT HAPPENS
AFTER WE DIE?

Todd looked away from me as he spoke and only checked my eyes every now and then to measure my level of skepticism.

"My family took my father's death very hard. Especially my mother," he began. "We have always been very logical people, so that makes this story even more difficult to tell."

Todd's father had been a deacon in his church for many years and only resigned after cancer had ravaged his body to the point that church work became impossible.

After he died, his family mourned together and attempted to transition into their lives without him. Todd went back to Alabama, his brother to Ohio and his mother to Tennessee.

Todd's mother called him one night the week after the funeral and told him a fantastic story. According to her, Todd's father had appeared to her just before she fell asleep and gave her a simple "thumbs up" sign before vanishing.

"I think he wants me to know that he's okay," she said to Todd.

Todd humored his mother and told her how glad he was she could now be at peace with her husband's death.

He placed the phone on the cradle and shook his head.

"Dad's death has really been difficult for her. Now she's seeing things," he thought.

About half an hour later, the phone rang again. This time Todd's brother, Jason, greeted him from the other end.

"I need to tell you something," Jason's voice trembled.

"I saw Dad. I know it sounds crazy, but he gave me a thumbs up and then he was gone."

"Have you talked to mom?" Todd asked.

"Not since the day before yesterday," Jason answered.

Todd didn't know what to think. He knew his family members were not liars, and, though people can be fooled by their imaginations, it was unlikely that two people on opposite sides of the country could imagine they saw the exact same thing within half an hour of each other.

Odds are you have heard stories similar to Todd's. You may even have one of your own (or maybe several).

I used to rationalize away such stories, conveniently brushing aside such claims as physical flukes, hallucinations, or outright lies. I don't recall having ever said that to the face of a self-proclaimed eyewitness, but I used one of those answers as a silver bullet to assure myself that I had been correctly taught concerning the world of the dead—that they were oblivious and transparent.

I'm certainly not saying that these events happen often. In fact, I think they are quite rare. But I don't think such events are impossible as I once did because I have learned otherwise from God's Word.

Alexander Campbell was a Bible scholar in the 1800's and holds my deepest respect because of his dedication to the study of God's Word. Though his opinion should not be equated with the Bible, I believe that anything he wrote is worth consideration.

In one of Alexander's theological speeches, he makes a very

interesting comment that is relative to our study of those of us who have passed away. He says:

> "But here we must pause; and, with this awful group of exasperated and malicious demons in our horizon, it is some relief to remember that there are many good spirits of our race, allied with ten thousand times ten thousand, and thousands of thousands, of angels of light."[1]

His wording is unique but his message is clear—"there are many good spirits of our race allied with" angels ministering to us.

Think about it and you'll agree with Campbell's words. Can you think of a time when a righteous dead person mentioned in the Bible *didn't know* what was happening on earth?

In addition to knowing events that took place on earth, they were concerned and even involved in some cases by bringing messages about the future.

A basic look at biblical references to the righteous dead shows that they are not unaware or censored from the events of our world.

Our first passage of interest comes from the Old Testament era. King Saul convinced the witch of Endor to bring Samuel from the dead because he thought Samuel could help him. But when Samuel appeared to Saul, he proved to be anything but helpful.

---

[1] *In addition to being available in religious libraries, at the time of this writing a transcript of this speech was available on the Internet at http://www.mun.ca/rels/restmov/texts/acampbell/mh1841/DEMON1.HTM*

"I am in great distress,' Saul said. 'The Philistines are fighting against me, and God has turned away from me. He no longer answers me, either by prophets or by dreams. So I have called on you to tell me what to do.'

Samuel said, 'Why do you consult me, now that the LORD has turned away from you and become your enemy? The LORD has done what he predicted through me. The LORD has torn the kingdom out of your hands and given it to one of your neighbors—to David. Because you did not obey the LORD or carry out his fierce wrath against the Amalekites, the LORD has done this to you today. The LORD will hand over both Israel and you to the Philistines, and tomorrow you and your sons will be with me. The LORD will also hand over the army of Israel to the Philistines.'" (1 Samuel 28:15-19)

Samuel knew about the war between Saul's army and the Philistines. Samuel's reply to Saul showed extensive knowledge of the situation because he used words like "now" and boldly said, *"The Lord has torn the kingdom out of your hands and given it to David."*

Not only did he know everything that was happening, but he told Saul he would not survive the next day of battle with the Philistines.

Samuel lived in the world of the dead, yet he knew exactly what was occurring on earth among his people. God revealed to Samuel what to say to Sau/

Our next example of interest comes from the New Testament. When Jesus attempted discussing his approaching death with Peter,

James and John, they showed very little support. In fact, Jesus became angry when Peter urged Him not to go through with it (Matthew 16:21-23).

After that, two teachers of the past named Moses and Elijah came to Jesus and offered Him words of encouragement concerning His impending sacrifice.

> *"As he was praying, the appearance of his face changed, and his clothes became as bright as a flash of lightning. Two men, Moses and Elijah, appeared in glorious splendor, talking with Jesus. They spoke about his departure, which he was about to bring to fulfillment at Jerusalem"* (Luke 9:29-31)

Notice that Luke says "two men" appeared to Jesus. Not two ghosts. Not two angels. Not two spirits. Two men. Two humans!

Note also that Luke says they appeared in "glorious splender." This wording is consistent with our new bodies being described as "glorious" in 1 Corinthians 15.

Moses and Elijah knew what was happening on earth; each knew that Jesus was about to fulfill the law and prophets and that His disciples weren't being supportive because they did not yet understand.

Samuel, Moses and Elijah lived with God in Paradise with all the other righteous dead yet they had ample knowledge of the current events on earth.

The third passage of interest tells of an occurrence in Heaven itself.

43

It tells of the righteous dead in <u>Heaven</u> praying for the events on earth. *? Paradise perhaps* John saw them and writes of what he saw.

> *"When he opened the fifth seal, I saw under the altar the souls of those who had been slain because of the word of God and the testimony they had maintained. They called out in a loud voice, 'How long, Sovereign Lord, holy and true, until you judge the inhabitants of the earth and avenge our blood?'*
>
> *Then each of them was given a white robe, and they were told to wait a little longer, until the number of their fellow servants and brothers who were to be killed as they had been was completed'"* (Revelation 6:9-11).

The martyrs were aware of the events on earth enough to know their deaths had yet to be avenged. They were told that vengeance would surely come but that they had to wait longer for it to occur.

Paradise The martyrs lived in the company of Samuel, Moses, Elijah and all the other righteous dead. Even though they were not on the earth, they were well aware of its events.

These three examples show that the righteous dead have knowledge of the happenings on earth. Can they actually see the earth or do they simply know because the information is provided in *Hades?* Heaven? The Bible does not tell us. But many Christians believe that Hebrews 12:1 teaches that the righteous dead have personal access to what occurs here. *Questionable*

"Therefore, since we are surrounded by such a great cloud of witnesses, let us throw off everything that hinders and the sin that so easily entangles, and let us run with perseverance the race marked out for us."

It's comforting to know that "a great cloud of witnesses" watch us and know what is happening in the present world. And because the saints in Revelation 6 prayed to God to avenge them on earth, I believe they pray to Him today as well. I'm sure they pray for more than just vengeance and I have no struggle believing that many of their prayers are for us.

I believe that there are people of God in Heaven praying for us. The passages discussed led me to believe that my family members who have gone to be with God know what happens here on earth. They are part of that "cloud of witnesses" surrounding me as I run my race. I haven't any doubt that in Heaven, they pray for me as well as other family and friends. Their prayers must be so much more powerful than ours without the weight of human doubt and the imbalance between our fallen bodies and spirits. *Comforting – but true?*

I wrote the following paragraphs in my book, *Seeing the Unseen*, concerning this topic and believe they summarize my beliefs regarding Christians who have died.

I strongly believe that the dead know what is happening here on earth. I believe that strongly enough that I'll ask you a favor. If for some reason I were to die soon, I want you to

we have been taught that our works are complete while living. It would be nice to think that we could pray for our loved ones. But think of Lazarus and the rich man.

take a message to my children for me. At my funeral con-
sole my three daughters with this chapter. Read my words
to them. Tell them I love them and I'll watch them throughout their lives. I'll hurt when they struggle. I'll rejoice in
their triumphs. I'll cry at their weddings.

Tell them that when they feel extra strength come from
God, their daddy is praying for them. Just because he now
lives in Heaven doesn't mean he's forgotten them.

Tell them I'll hurt with them as they learn the tough side
of life. I'll swell with pride at their successes. I'll gaze lov-
ingly at any of my grandchildren they bear, [just as I watch
with wonder those God has already given me].

When you tell my mentally-challenged daughter,
Angela, she'll have the toughest time understanding what
you mean—and the easiest time believing it once she sorts
it out in her way. Her simplicity keeps her closer to Heaven
than the rest of us anyway.[2]

those that are asleep
I Cor. 15:6, :18
I Thes. 4:13, 15

IF THE DEAD ARE AWARE OF OUR STRUGGLES, HOW IS IT HEAVEN?

I remember sitting at the funeral of my Aunt Darlene. Though
the tremendous pain of cancer had invaded the last few years of her

---

[2]*Seeing the Unseen: Preparing Yourself for Spiritual Warfare by Joe Beam —Revised and Updated, page 299. West Monroe, LA: Howard Publishing, 2000.*

life, she always seemed to have a smile on her face and an unusually pleasant attitude. She was indeed the "salt of the earth." I miss her very much.

As I sat at her funeral, a song that her family requested played for the solemn crowd. The song is one that you may have heard. It's called, "Holes in the Floor of Heaven," sung by Vince Gill.

If you've listened to that song, I have no doubt you were touched by its words. As you might expect by the title, the song tells the story of loved ones in Heaven, watching over us. Especially touching about this song is that the story is of a young child asking about his mother in Heaven.

While listening to that song at Darlene's funeral, it seemed stingingly depressing yet strangely hopeful. She had left behind two sons. One was very young, and I ached when I thought of how he had only had a few years with his mother and would now be facing the rest of his childhood without her. Yet the song reinforced the truth that she would be watching over him. She wouldn't miss his first love, his graduation or the birth of his children. She will be a witness to all those events if she chooses (and I'm sure she will).

I'm not saying it will be the same as if she had continued living on this earth. It's not the same. It's not even ideal. But I do believe that God took some of the sting out of death by providing a future for those who die.

A question usually surfaces from the discussion of loved ones being aware even after death. Often I'll hear, "But how can the Bible say there won't be crying or pain in Heaven? Surely, if our loved ones are aware of the bad things that happen to us, it wouldn't really be Heaven." *It isn't heaven! It is hades!*

I certainly understand the reasoning behind the question, but I think it is asked without certain points being considered.

After all, God is well aware of what is happening on earth, yet it is still Heaven for Him.

The angels are also aware of what is happening on earth, yet it is still Heaven for them.

The Bible even tells us that angels see the horror of Hell (Revelation 14:10), but it does not take away from the fact that they are in Heaven.

True for Jesus When Jesus lived on earth, He mourned and grieved for the people on earth (Matthew 23:37-39; John 11:33-36), but that does not mean that He is now incapable of mourning for us in Heaven when we encounter life's troubles.

In Revelation 21, the Bible does tell us there will not be crying or mourning in Heaven, but it tells us that all of that will be wiped out when *"the old order of things has been passed away."* Our loved ones are in waiting on the fulfillment of the resurrection of the dead, as well as the end of this earth. Until "the old order of things has been passed away," there are still reasons to mourn. But I suspect they will be blessed with a much clearer perspective of "the big picture." God is there to comfort them, and they understand that certain things must happen before we can be there with them.

There certainly are "holes in the floor of Heaven." At least in that parents can see their children, children can see their parents, a spouse can see the one left behind, and friends can see friends. What happens on earth is still very important to them because we are here. They are not as far away from us as we think.

WHERE WILL THE DEAD BE BEFORE THE RESURRECTION?

The natural order of things would seem to place this section before the discussion of our resurrection bodies.

However, it seemed to me that we couldn't discuss this subject without first establishing the concept of the resurrection body and how that body will be human and physical. Now that we have established that, we can discuss what happens immediately at death.

There are different views concerning the existence of the dead before the resurrection.

One view is that the souls of the dead hibernate or sleep while waiting on the resurrection. It would be like saving a computer file onto a floppy disk or CD-ROM. The file would be saved until needed again, and then it would be retrieved. In this case, the soul would be saved in the mind of God and then revived on the day of resurrection.

I find this theory very difficult to accept because of the many examples in the Bible of the dead being conscious, active and aware (1 Sam. 28:15-19; Luke 9:29-31; 16:22-31; Rev. 6:9-11). Also, in Matthew 22:32 Jesus said to the Sadducees, *"But about the resurrection of the dead—have you not read what God said to you, 'I am the God of Abraham, the God of Isaac, and the God of Jacob'? He*

49

is not the God of the dead but of the living." Jesus listed Abraham, Isaac and Jacob among the living. He didn't say they were in limbo, unaware or filed away somewhere. He called them "the living."

Another theory is that we will be bodiless spirits roaming the earth until the day of resurrection. Because of scriptures that place the dead in Heaven (paradise) with God (Luke 6:19-31; 23:43; Revelation 6:11), I cannot accept that theory either.

Based on my study of Scripture, I believe that immediately after death the human spirit leaves the body and goes to either Heaven or Hell. We will not lose conscious existence after death, but we will take up where we left off in Heaven or in Hell. Our souls do not sleep or experience a period of unawareness while waiting on Heaven or Hell. The Day of Judgment comes for each one of us when our body dies. Those who have not died when God raises the dead and gives them their new bodies will be judged at that time.

Someone might use 1 Thessalonians 4:13-17 as a proof text for the theory of "soul sleep." Let's carefully examine this passage:

"Brothers, we do not want you to be ignorant about those who fall asleep, or to grieve like the rest of men, who have no hope. We believe that Jesus died and rose again and so we believe that God will bring with Jesus those who have fallen asleep in him. According to the Lord's own word, we tell you that we who are still alive, who are left till the coming of the Lord, will certainly not precede those who have fallen asleep. For the Lord himself will come down from the

Heaven, with a loud command, with the voice of the archangel and with the trumpet call of God, and the dead in Christ will rise first. After that, we who are still alive and are left will be caught up together with them in the clouds to meet the Lord in the air. And so we will be with the Lord forever. Therefore encourage each other with these words."

This Scripture mentions several complex issues. In determining the meaning of the phrase, "fallen asleep," we must also consider the other passages that deal with the condition of the dead before the return of Jesus. Based on other Biblical teachings that we've mentioned previously, I think it is consistent to say that this passage refers to the outward appearance of the body that has died. It appears to be asleep in that the eyes are closed and the body is completely still. The earthly physical part of us "sleeps" until it is reunited with our spirit at the resurrection. The spiritual part of us relocates to a conscious existence in Heaven (if we are God's children).

Because the book of Revelation references human beings talking and worshipping in Heaven before the resurrection, it could be at that state that the dead have some sort of a temporary body. Because humans are both spiritual and physical (Genesis 2:7), a temporary body would allow us to maintain human qualities.

Others have suggested that during that time we will be spirits without bodies until the resurrection, when our former bodies are raised and changed. I believe there to be a fatal flaw to this argument in the parable Jesus told about the rich man and Lazarus (Luke 16:19-31).

Jesus noted that the rich man requested relief from his pain. The rich man asked for Lazarus to "dip the tip of his finger in water and cool" his "tongue." An interesting request from a bodiless spirit, wouldn't you say?

And remember, the story of the rich man and Lazarus is *not* in the setting of Heaven *after* the resurrection of the dead. The story says that the rich man begged for Lazarus to be allowed to go back to earth and tell the rich man's friends and family to change so that they would not end up in torment like him. This tells us that Jesus was describing an event just after the death of two humans and before the resurrection placing all humans in either Heaven or Hell.

I have listened to some preachers dismiss this passage because Jesus told it as a parable, that the story may or may not have been based on an actual event but was meant to make a point, like a hypothetical situation. However, I believe that Jesus would not mislead us by His stories nor is it in His character to be fake, dishonest or inaccurate. His parables provided extremely powerful points because ordinary people could connect with them. Why would Jesus tell stories using impossible or fictional scenarios? It just doesn't make sense. The Bible says that God is *"not the God of confusion"* (1 Cor. 14:33 NKJV), so why would He tell stories that include imaginary, impossible events and expect us to determine when He was correct or erroneous? I don't believe He did. I believe His stories were realistic possibilities used to help us put our lives in perspective.

After all, in the story of the sower in Mark 4, if Jesus would have added absurd and impossible events to the story, it would have lost its point. What if Jesus said that the sower planted seed to grow feathers? Not only would it have been factually impossible, because feathers cannot be grown from a seed, but Jesus would have lost credibility with His audience for making such an inaccurate statement.

Therefore, I believe that we can derive from the story of the rich man and Lazarus and the story of the apostles recognizing Moses and Elijah at the Transfiguration that we will exist in some kind of body before the return of Jesus when our old bodies will be used as seed for our new bodies built to last for eternity. After all, in Matthew 22:32, Jesus quoted God in saying that God was *"the God of Isaac, and the God of Jacob. He is not the God of the dead but of the living."*

Living men have bodies.

THE VALUE OF THIS LIFE

It's common for some to speak disparagingly about this life in an attempt to sound spiritual. They act as though this life is simply an ongoing mistake that forces their eyes to open each morning. This viewpoint, like the idea that our body is simply a dungeon trapping our spirits, may sound poetic and righteous, but that does not make it so.

This spirit that he talks about is the spirit of life. Without this spirit the body would be dead.

If we look at the life of Jesus, we see a very different picture. He healed people physically, as well as spiritually. If this life really didn't matter, why did He bother healing people physically? Why didn't He just say, "All that matters is the next life! I don't want to waste my time on the physical." *What matters is how you live this life.*

The spirit returns to God (who gave it) and the body returns to dust as stated in the Bible

53

Furthermore, Jesus brought two people back from death. Lazarus walked out of the tomb after four days (John 11:43-44), and Jesus caused the dead daughter of "the ruler" to open her eyes and sit up (Mark 9:23-25).

If this life did not have importance, why did Jesus bother to bring them back from the afterlife to the worthlessness of this life?

This is not to say that this life is as important as the eternal life we will experience afterwards. Colossians 3:2 says, *"Set your mind on the things above ... "*

Yet at the same time, the Bible says, *"If anyone does not provide for his relatives, and especially for his immediate family, he has denied the faith and is worse than an unbeliever"* (1 Tim. 5:8).

The excuse to not providing for family could be, "But Lord, this life doesn't matter. All I could think about was Heaven and was so consumed by it that I was unable to provide for my family." *trash!*

God says that person has "denied the faith and is worse than an unbeliever" because he failed to do his duty by neglecting his responsibility to those who depended on him for life. Clearly, God expects us to take this life seriously and to assign it the level of importance it is due as a gift and an assignment from Him. *Absolutely*

As with the relationship between our bodies and our spirits, we must maintain balance. We must fulfill our responsibilities on earth, while at the same time fulfilling our responsibilities to the next life. Colossians says, *"Whatever you do, work at it with all your heart, as working for the Lord, not for men, since you know that you will receive an inheritance from the Lord as a reward. It is the Lord*

Christ you are serving" (Col. 3:23-24).

We should consider life a service to God. We are to live with a higher standard than the rest of the world. While, the rest of the world works for bosses, we are to work at our jobs as if for God and do our very best for Him, no matter what we do. If we are lazy when it's time to work, we aren't only short-changing our employer, we are short-changing God. He gave us life and expects us to honestly use the talents and abilities He gave us. *True*

God expects us to value this life because He gave it to us. Consider that this life will provide memories that we will remember for eternity. Don't take it for granted, but at the same time, remember that God has even more awaiting us.

In the next chapter, we discuss what it will be like to live in Heaven with God for eternity. I believe we will find many similarities to life here on earth, as well as some great differences and improvements. Keep in mind as you read the next chapter, and throughout the rest of this book, that your life is important and that you are not just in "a waiting room." What you do here will affect eternity and your life here is just as much part of God's Will as eternity in Heaven. *He is right on*

The Resurrection Body
I Cor. 15:35-44

WHERE IS HEAVEN?

I'll admit it. I've always been a Trekkie. From a young age I wanted to go boldly where no man had gone before, just as the crew aboard the Star Trek Enterprise did on my TV. Captain Kirk lived out some of my dreams as he landed on distant planets and flew past the countless stars in our massive universe. When I was in kindergarten, my parents, friends and teachers knew I wanted to be an astronaut when I grew up. My parents took me to the Space and Rocket Center in Huntsville, Alabama, more times than I can remember, and I actually liked the freeze-dried "Astronaut Ice Cream" that we bought with each visit.

I have yet to speak to anyone who doesn't have at least a pleasant curiosity about the universe. Why should we not be interested in the work of our Father's hands?

Today we call it outer space. In Paul's day, they called it the "second heaven." They considered the atmosphere around the earth to be the first heaven, the second heaven held the stars, and the third Heaven served as the location of God's kingdom.

When the biblical text says *heaven*, it might mean any of those three areas. We need to know which "heaven" the Bible describes before we make conclusions.

Usually when the Bible uses the plural of heaven, it is referring to either the clouds or outer space. When it is singular, it is usually referring to the location of God's kingdom. But that's not always the case, especially when considering the differences in versions.

SOME EXAMPLES OF THE WORD HEAVEN

Heaven is often translated as *air* by many of the modern versions whereas the older versions and the New King James version of the Bible uses the word *heaven*.

For example, Job 35:10-11 reads:

"But no one says, 'Where is God my Maker, who gives songs in the night, who teaches more to us than to the beasts of the earth and makes us wiser than the birds of the air?'"

Air is the word of choice for the New International Version and the New Revised Standard while the King James and New King James say *heaven*.

The second use of *heaven*, what we call outer space, is translated as expanse of the *sky* in Genesis 1:14 by the New International Version, as *dome of the sky* by the New Revised Standard, as *firmament of the heaven* by the King James Version, and as *firmament of the heavens* by the New King James Version.

The third *heaven*, the location of God's kingdom, is most often translated as *Heaven*. An example is 2 Chronicles 7:14 which reads, *"If my people, who are called by my name, will humble themselves and pray and seek my face and turn from their wicked ways, then will I hear from Heaven and forgive their sin and will heal their land."*

When Jesus pardoned the thief on the cross and told him that they would see each other in Heaven that day, His word for *Heaven* is translated as *paradise* by all the major versions of today.

GOD'S KINGDOM

When you bought this book, you were probably assuming that my use of the word *Heaven* in the title referred to the location of God's kingdom. And you were correct. But it is important to know which of the three heavens the Bible refers to in certain passages. Don't necessarily assume the Bible is referring to God's kingdom when it uses the word "heaven." Consider the context of the passage in which the word is used before arriving at a conclusion.

HEAVEN'S LOCATION

Though it might seem harsh, be very leery of anyone who claims to know the current location of Heaven. The Bible simply does not tell us, and the universe is much too vast for us to pinpoint an exact or approximate location.

I can, however, make an assumption that Heaven is somewhere

in the universe because when Jesus left for Heaven, He ascended. When we travel "up," on earth we are really going "out." Jesus went into outer space on His way to Heaven. That's about all we can presume concerning the present location of Heaven, but as you'll see in the following chapter, Heaven will one day relocate.

You see, it seems clear to me from the Bible that the future location of Heaven will be on the New Earth.

LIFE IN THE
NEW WORLD

"'As the new heavens and the New Earth that I make will endure before me,' says the Lord, 'so will your name and descendants endure'" (Isaiah 66:22).

For some of you, life in Heaven may sometimes sound oxymoronic because it is something that comes after death. Why should we discuss it? Why dwell on what happens in the afterlife? Isn't Heaven just the parting gift for dying? Isn't it simply to give us a little more peace when death's bed finally comes?

I must admit, for a time, I refused to think about Heaven except when I thought of a deceased loved one. I didn't want to imagine that person lying in a grave and I didn't want to think I'd never see them again. So Heaven made a great distraction. I could simply stick them in a vague, dream-like Heaven in my mind and take them out whenever I chose to entertain the idea that they weren't completely dead. I made Heaven blurry and mysterious enough that I didn't have to deal with what may or may not be true. That way I could hold off death and the thought of death as long as I possibly could.

Why?

What about death terrifies us so much? Is that fear simply a natural instinct placed within us to keep us alive as long as possible? Is it because we don't really believe in an afterlife? Is it because we aren't confident of our standing with God? Is it that we're afraid of losing all that we've worked for and having to start over? Or is it simply the fear the unknown?

We've all struggled with at least one of those fears when thinking about Heaven.

It is perfectly natural to try to avoid death, even if we believe Heaven waits on the other side. We were created to despise and run from death at all costs and, if we weren't, I can't imagine how the human species would still exist. We've probably all been in life or death situations, and the "fight or flight" adrenaline rush gave us the extra focus and strength needed to save our own lives or the life of another.

I'll be very honest with you. I don't want to die. I want to live for years and years to come. I want to experience special moments with my family and friends. And that's okay. If God didn't want us to enjoy life, He wouldn't have created us to do so. And if He didn't want us in this life anymore, He would decide to return right now and put an end to it all. That means God's timing is not yet complete. I have no right to interrupt or "help Him along" with the process of taking me to Heaven.

I believe that this life is important. It matters and should be appreciated and valued. Why? Perhaps an illustration will help me explain.

As a teenager, I wanted little more than to drive a car. I watched as my friends turned driving age and could barely contain my anxiousness to grasp the steering wheel of a powerful, modern-day machine.

You can imagine my frustration when my time came to drive and my dad chose a church parking lot for my training.

I flippantly made the turns, stops and maneuvers he required until he offered some wisdom for my consideration.

"Son," he began, "if you can't prove to me that you can handle this vehicle at slow speeds in a small parking lot, what would make me think you can safely navigate it at high speeds with other cars within only a few feet of your life? Furthermore, if you won't take training seriously, how can I know that you'll ever take driving seriously?"

We see this principle throughout life. It's usually the minor leagues before the majors. It's basic training before active wartime assignments. And it's *earth* before eternity with God.

On this earth, we learn many lessons that will be valuable in Heaven. We learn how to work, study, and, most importantly, how to have faith in God. All those lessons will be useful in Heaven.

GOD WILL STILL BE GOD

There is a popular perception that says we will know everything there is to know when we get to Heaven. This belief persists despite the fact that it is widely accepted that humans die without perfect knowledge and that God alone is perfect in knowledge. The assumption is that all this will be given to us at the resurrection of the dead and the return of Jesus Christ. Let's further examine that idea.

WILL WE KNOW EVERYTHING IN HEAVEN?

Some have said as much, but only God knows everything and, therefore, is omniscient. If we also knew everything, we would be equal to God. That will never be the case. To see clearly (1 Cor. 13:12) and have a greater understanding is one thing, but to be omniscient like God is another. The angels in Heaven don't know everything and neither will glorified humans who live in Heaven.

We will, however, be constantly learning. Heaven won't be a stagnant world, but it will be a fresh, stimulating and challenging frontier where we will develop an ever-deepening understanding of God's greatness (Revelation 4 and 5, Eph. 2:7). We will continue to grow, change, learn and mature without sin to weigh down or deter us, and we wouldn't want it any other way.

Can you imagine a world in which you knew everything? A world where every mystery had been solved and no adventure or dream remained possible? Humans would be miserable in such a world because we were created by God to learn, study, think, experiment, theorize, discuss, and examine. How incredibly boring it would be to have every challenge and question removed from our existence. We could never look forward to knowing something new and fresh. We just weren't cut out for that.

Only God has the capacity to know absolutely everything there is to know and not crack under the pressure. He has that capacity because He is infinite. There is no end to Him. Only God lives without anything new or unexpected. Why? Because He is the Creator, and we are the created. He is the painter, and we are the painting. We are in His world, not He in ours. He is the potter, we are the clay. He is the teacher, we are the students.

We weren't created to have all knowledge and understanding, but God has always had it and always will.

IS THIS WORLD MY HOME?

You might be humming the words to a popular Christian song after reading the title to this section.

> "This world is not my home, I'm just [passing] through. My treasures are laid up somewhere beyond the blue. The angels beckon me from Heaven's open door and I can't feel at home in this world anymore."

I remember singing that song in church as a small child. The words reminded me that this life might be tough, and even terrible at times, but one day God would welcome me into a place that wasn't earth where all of my dreams would come true.

That sounded wonderful, but something didn't add up.

Why would God put me on this earth, only to take me to another place entirely when my time here ended? Why two places? Why did He put humans here in the first place if we belonged somewhere else?

I never asked those questions to anyone growing up, but I listened to the answers given when others asked similar questions. Sometimes the answers consisted of the old Gnostic philosophies. The explanation would be that we really didn't belong in a body to begin with, and when Jesus returned, God would rescue our spirits from our bodies to take those spirits to Heaven where they belonged.

As I learned the basics of the Bible, I added to my list of questions concerning the theory of Heaven that people generally seemed to accept. The very first book of the Bible triggered one question: Why did God work to develop a place for us if it was the wrong place for us to begin with? Why did He create a human if humans would one day become extinct and morphed into another being altogether? Bottom line: If God considered His creation to be "good" upon completion (Genesis 1:31), why would He change His mind at a later time? Why did God create Adam and Eve to live forever on earth as humans but then decide we would be better off as nonhumans?

As you know from previous chapters, I don't believe that we will be nonhumans in the afterlife. I don't believe that God mistakenly created humans and placed them on earth to live forever as a mistake.

The fact that He originally intended for us to live on earth forever as humans is very important to this study because we are able to see the design as God originally intended.

Adam and Eve were not supposed to die. They were supposed to be stewards of the earth forever, and God supplied them with "the Tree of Life" so that they would be able to live forever *as humans*.

The Bible shows us the lingering effects of the Tree of Life on humans as it began to wear off. Adam still lived to be over nine hundred years old! Slowly but certainly, the lifespan of humans fell until now we live to be between eighty and one hundred years old.

Since God planned for humans to live forever on earth in the beginning, He would be totally giving up by taking us somewhere else. He didn't make a mistake by creating human beings and the earth. Clearly, His plans were for us to live forever on earth. We were the ones who messed it up (Genesis 3).

Satan tempted Adam and Eve with an offer they thought they couldn't refuse—godhood. He didn't offer them the ability to create galaxies or life forms in mere seconds, but something almost as tempting—knowledge.

"You'll be like God and know what He knows" he hissed (Genesis 3:5).

When Adam and Eve proved they couldn't resist Satan's offer, God gave them their space, allowing them to actually be the gods of their own lives (Genesis 3:22-24).

God basically said, "You want to be a god? Go be one! Apparently you think you can handle it. I'll just take back my garden paradise and turn the control of the earth over to you. You'll be in charge of getting food to grow from the earth. You'll be in charge of keeping peace among all the other 'human gods.' And while you're at it, be god over your health and life. Let me know how that goes."

You see, humans cannot sustain themselves without God. We

have failed miserably at the task of being our own god and that fact becomes painfully clear when we pass by cemeteries and hospitals. We have knowledge of good and evil like God and are in the very image of God Himself. We are able to procreate new life and have a spirit within us like God. There are many traits that we share with God, but they aren't enough. Our shortcomings are much too great.

We are unable to force the earth to do our will. Sure, we get close by growing food out of the earth, drilling for oil to use, clearing forests for roads and buildings, and having some control over other life forms on the earth. But the wind and water do not obey our very words as they did when God Himself calmly demanded they stop all the commotion (Luke 8:22-25). And we have to protect ourselves from the heat and cold by seeking some form of shelter.

Where we fall terribly short is an area over which we have very little control—our lives. We can't sustain ourselves forever. Only God can provide and maintain eternal life, and we can't even scratch the surface.

Truly, we make miserable gods.

As Christians, we are called to step down from the throne in order to be subject to the only true God. Perhaps the message of the Bible could be summed up in one sentence: Humans can't be God, but *God* can.

Because God is a perfect gentleman, He won't force Himself onto the throne of your life. He doesn't have an ego issue that requires your loyalty to give Him a sense of self-worth. Though He doesn't have to, God allows us to choose our ruler.

God's message from the Bible is, "If you so choose, I'll be your God again as I was in the beginning. I'll provide you with eternal life—again. I'll restore fellowship between you and me. I'll take control of the earth again, when the time is right.

The earth. The "New Earth" for the new human. God intended for us to live on an earth where He served as God, not one where we live separate from Him and slowly watch ourselves die. That's not God's will.

This world was our home until we distorted and stained it, but God does not believe in dead ends for those who are His. Just as God washed us clean and made us new, He will renew the earth and restore it to His original intent—to be a perfect home for us, a home where He will live with us as our God. The Bible tells this to us:

> *"Then I saw a new heaven and a new earth, for the first heaven and the first earth had passed away, and there was no longer any sea. I saw the Holy City, the New Jerusalem, coming down out of Heaven from God, prepared as a bride beautifully dressed for her husband. And I heard a loud voice from the throne saying, 'Now the dwelling of God is with men, and he will live with them. They will be his people, and God himself will be with them and be their God'"*
> (Revelation 21:1-3).

You see, it's not that we "die and go to Heaven," it's that God raises us from the dead and sends Heaven to the New Earth.

This concept of God making His home with man is further supported with the words of Jesus in John 14:23:

"If anyone loves me, he will obey my teaching. My Father will love him, and we will come to him and make our home with him."

WHAT WILL THE NEW EARTH BE LIKE?

Like our new bodies, earth will keep the things that make it earth. The New Earth will contain trees, rivers, mountains and vegetation.

Just as we might maintain identifying marks in Heaven such as scars and physical features, the New Earth may very well have some, if not all, of the natural wonders that is has now.

It could be that one day you stand with a friend on a mountain on the New Earth and say, "Do you remember when we hiked up this mountain when it was the Old Earth and saw that beautiful field? Let's go see it now!"

You see, just as our current bodies will be a "seed" for our new bodies, this earth will be seed for the New Earth on which we will live.

As C.S. Lewis said, ". . . the hills and valleys of Heaven will be to those you now experience not as a copy is to an original, nor as a substitute is to the genuine article, but as the flower to the root, or the diamond to the coal." (C.S. Lewis, Letter to Malcolm: Chiefly on Prayer. New York: Harcourt Brace Jovanovich, 1963. Page 84)

If you want clues to what Heaven will be like, all you have to do is look around. Heaven will be located on the New Earth with us, and we will be able to live in the paradise God intended for us all along. Just as God redeemed us from sin, He will redeem the earth from its curse.

Many theories and books on Heaven attempt to be deeply philosophical and profound when assessing Heaven. To some it seems too easy to place humans on a real planet where they will have real bodies, but God is the one who chose the earth as the perfect place for us in the beginning. Though it is only a decaying remnant of what it once was, we can still be taken back at its incredible beauty. Truly, God created it as a perfect paradise for us because, even in its cursed, dying state, it beams of majesty and splendor.

We can have a very good idea of what the New Earth will be like because the Bible tells us about the earth before sin's contamination (Genesis 1 and 2). The New Earth will be a restoration of the current earth to the paradise of God's original plan, and He will make His home here with us when that happens.

If you still aren't convinced that this earth will be the location of our heavenly reward, consider what Peter wrote in Acts 3:21:

"He [Jesus] must remain in Heaven until the time comes for God to restore everything, as he promised long ago through his holy prophets."

Note that this passage says God will restore everything. Because we have never lived in a disembodied, otherworldly state, for God to take us to such a place would not qualify as a restoration at all.

The reward in the afterlife for Christians is God restoring the earth, humans and the entire physical universe to His original design.

Peter not only learned of the restoration concept through the prophets, he heard it from Jesus Himself. When Peter told Jesus that the disciples had left everything to follow Him, he wanted a reward or a pat on the back from Jesus. Jesus didn't scold or rebuke Him but said:

> *"I tell you the truth, at the renewal of all things, when the Son of Man sits on his glorious throne, you who have followed me will also sit on twelve thrones, judging the twelve tribes of Israel"* (Matthew 19:27-28).

Did you notice the Lord's choice of words? He didn't say "at the annihilation of all things" or "at the departure of all things" but "at the *renewal* of all things."

Christ's statement distinguishes between two deeply different theologies. God created humans to live on the earth. That is what Christ secured at His resurrection—a renewed humanity on a renewed earth with a renewed relationship with God.[3]

The belief that the Heaven God plans for us will be unearthly and nonhuman is simply unbiblical. God made the earth for us to live on and made us to live on the earth. God bought His creation

---

[3]*Heaven by Randy Alcorn, page 911.*

back; He didn't go back to the drawing board. That is why it is called *redemption.*

If we lost the earth forever and our bodies turned to ghosts in Heaven, then redemption wouldn't have been accomplished at all but, instead, total surrender to the enemy!

As Anthony Hoekema says, "If God would have to annihilate the present cosmos, Satan would have won a great victory . . . Satan would have succeeded in so devastatingly corrupting the present cosmos and the present earth that God could do nothing with it but to blot it totally out of existence. But Satan did not win such a victory. On the contrary, Satan has been decisively defeated. God will reveal the full dimensions of that defeat when He shall renew this very earth on which Satan deceived mankind and finally banish from it all the results of Satan's evil machinations." (*The Bible and the Future.* Grand Rapids: Eerdmans, 1979. Page 280)

IS THIS MY FATHER'S WORLD?

I believe that one of the reasons some Christians have difficulty understanding that Heaven will not only be physical but actually on earth is because of passages that tell us to distance ourselves from the world.

John wrote, *"Do not love the world or anything in the world"* (1 John 2:15), and yet he also wrote, *"For God so loved the world that he gave his one and only Son"* (John 3:16).

James echoes John's call to defy the world:

> *"Don't you know that friendship with the world is hatred toward God? Anyone who chooses to be a friend of the world becomes an enemy of God"* (James 4:4).

But how can we not love a world that God created for us? Paul says in 1 Corinthians 7:31 that *"this world in its present form is passing away"* due to the curse placed upon it because of sin. We are not to love the earth *in its present form* because it has been distorted from God's original intent.

For our study on Heaven and the New Earth, take Paul's lead by attaching the phrase "in its present form" onto those passages that tell us to withdraw from the world. This will help us understand them in their context.

For example:

> *"Don't you know that friendship with the world [in its present form] is hatred toward God? Anyone who chooses to be a friend of the world [in its present form] becomes an enemy of God"* (James 4:4).

Compare the concept to former communist Russia. Those who wanted change both loved and hated their country. They hated it because of the large, life-controlling government that persecuted so many. But, they loved it for what it used to be and could be again.

In fact, with many native Russians, it was love that propelled them to defy the communist-controlled Soviets and led many to rebel in order to bring about change. In the same way, we are to defy the earth *in its present form* because we know that God made it to be a much better place than it is now.

We are to reject the world in its present form in the same way that Paul said we are to reject a brother or sister in Christ when they are continually and willfully sinful (1 Corinthians 5). Not because we expected him to live a perfect and sinless life but in order to bring him back to repentance. The only hope of restoring him to God, according to Paul, is by rejecting his sinful activity. He has to know that children of God reject his behavior because, as God's child, he is supposed to be pure and set apart (2 Thessalonians 3:6). He is called to be an example of holiness, not a participant in paganism.

At the same time, we are to be patient and gentle with him when he acknowledges that he is being overcome by a specific sin and wants to be delivered. We are waiting on God to deliver the earth so that one day fellowship will be restored.

It's in our nature to love the world because God put it in us, but after the fall, many things changed. Christians are asked to temporarily go against our very nature, just as a father is asked to go against his nature by disciplining a child. Fathers don't want to see their children in pain, but they will sometimes force themselves to temporarily cause them pain for their long-term, greater good.

Our temporary rejection of this world is for the long-term greater good. We reject what goes against God, not only to bring glory to God out of the ashes of this fallen world, but to bring glory to God in the New Earth by bringing as many with us as possible.

THERE IS MUCH TO BE DONE IN HEAVEN

I know a very wealthy man who recently re-entered the job market. He had retired in his mid-thirties with more money than most people will see in a lifetime but wanted to return to work.

I'm sure some of you are reacting the same way I did when I heard. You're thinking, "What an idiot! The poor baby couldn't take a life of having anything he wanted and getting to sleep late every day?!"

But as I began to have more and more contact with him, I realized that he still had the demeanor of a man on a permanent vacation. He didn't seem to show the stress of running a business or staying up late to finish projects.

At first, I thought it might be the wealth he had continued to build, but I slowly realized that his life exemplified a principle of human nature that we often forget—the desire to be productive.

We all want to accomplish something worthwhile. We may not be enthusiastic about accomplishing things at our job because our interests are elsewhere, but if we are doing something that interests us and provides us with a sense of satisfaction when we are finished, we are experiencing one of the joys God programmed into us.

Humans were made to work.

From building houses to giving speeches, we all have different services to offer our fellow man.

And in looking to Heaven, it seems God does not separate work from paradise. He created the Garden of Eden as a paradise, yet required work from Adam and Eve (Genesis 2:15). It was no less paradise because humans worked.

When God restores the earth to His original intent, we'll be working again, but it won't be like the work we do now. Because of the curse, work became frustrating and repetitive.

God said, *"Cursed is the ground because of you; through painful toil you will eat of it all the days of your life. It will produce thorns and thistles for you, and you will eat the plants of the field. By the sweat of your brow you will eat your food"* (Genesis 3:17-19).

Work on the New Earth will not be such drudgery.

"No longer will there be any curse. The throne of God and of the Lamb will be in the city and his servants will serve him" (Revelation 22:3).

We will serve Him by ruling with Him.

That may sound odd to you because it is not something Christians talk about often. It's not a popular topic from the pulpit. It sounds far too politically incorrect to say, "One day Christians will rule the earth with God." It's not politically correct, but that doesn't make it untrue.

> *"Do you not know that the saints will judge the world? And if you are to judge the world, are you not competent to judge trivial cases? Do you not know that we will judge angels?"* (1 Corinthians 6:2)

> *"[I]f we endure, we will also reign with him"* (2 Timothy 2:12).

> *"To him who overcomes, I will give the right to sit with me on my throne, just as I overcame and sat down with my Father on his throne"* (Revelation 3:21).

In fact, in the beginning God told Adam and Eve to *"fill the earth and subdue it. Rule over the fish of the sea and the birds of the air and over every living creature that moves on the ground"* (Genesis 1:28).

On the New Earth, Jesus will be the King, and we will be His royal servants. We will rule with Him as active participants in His Kingdom.

God's children will carry out what He first appointed Adam and Eve to do.

> *"They will reign for ever and ever"* (Revelation 22:5).

We will reign with God in His Kingdom. It might sound

extreme and far-fetched, but it's been there all along.

"Then the King will say to those on his right, 'Come, you who are blessed by my Father; take your inheritance, the kingdom prepared for you since the creation of the world'" (Matthew 25:34).

"Blessed are the meek, for they will inherit the earth" (Matthew 5:5).

"Be faithful, even to the point of death, and I will give you the crown of life" (Revelation 2:10).

A crown? Who wears a crown but a king or ruler?

"[Y]ou have redeemed us to God by Your blood out of every tribe and tongue and people and nation, and have made us kings and priests to our God; and we shall reign on the earth" (Revelation 5:9-10).

We will be kings and priests, but how? The Bible is not as clear concerning this, but doesn't leave us without clues.

The Bible tells us that God's Kingdom on the New Earth will include celebration and feasting (Luke 14). Poverty and war will not exist because the Bread of Life and Prince of Peace will be King.

"See, your king comes to you righteous and having salvation . . . He will proclaim peace to the nations. His rule will extend from sea to sea and from the River to the ends of the earth" (Zechariah 9:9-10).

We will be rulers under Jesus, the King of kings. Perhaps some of us will rule towns, cities, states, even countries on the New Earth. We will be responsible for the care and upkeep of certain areas and lands, some of which we may actually own in terms of being the primary decision maker.

But who will we rule? In some cases, we will rule or supervise each other. Matthew 5:19, Luke 7:28 and other passages suggest that we will have different ranks or levels of responsibility in God's Kingdom on the New Earth.

"Anyone who breaks one of the least of these commandments and teaches others to do the same will be called least in the Kingdom of Heaven, but whoever practices and teaches these commands will be called great in the Kingdom of Heaven" (Matthew 5:19).

"I tell you, among those born of women there is no one greater than John; yet the one who is least in the kingdom of God is greater than he" (Luke 7:28).

Our society's greatest fear seems to be having another person viewed as superior or better in some way. But God decides what rank we may have and we will gratefully accept any position in the Lord's Kingdom.

Students confronted one of my high-school Bible teachers about these passages, and to this day, I appreciate his reply. He said, "I'll be happy even if I have the last spot on the *floor* to sit."

After all, Heaven is still Heaven.

The Bible also tells us that there will be different levels of punishments for those who aren't God's children (Matthew 23:13, Luke 11:23-24).

We won't be stale, mindless robots in Heaven but, as we have already mentioned, will keep our personalities and idiosyncrasies. Some of us are more cut out to take charge of certain aspects of a venture, while others are more gifted in carrying out the details of missions and projects. Remember, even in Heaven the clay does not question its Potter (Isaiah 45:9).

It's possible we will not only be ruling over areas on the New Earth.

God is a Creator by heart. We live on one planet in a gigantic universe of billions of other planets and stars that are the result of God's endless creativity.

Why does the Bible tell us that we will not only receive a New Earth, but a new universe? How very interesting! What would be the point of having a new universe with all that space just sitting idle? It's certainly possible that humans could be involved in some projects in other areas of the universe.

And you thought "Heaven talk" was boring.

CHAPTER 6

WILL ANIMALS BE IN HEAVEN?

I cried as I helped my brother dig his grave. I'd always hoped that "Ole Yella" and "Turner and Hooch" would remain trapped in Hollywood instead of becoming real life.

Bullet was a boxer bulldog who couldn't have been more likable. He didn't have a temper and enjoyed being with the four humans who made him part of their family.

It might sound silly, but his collar had a metal tag that included our last name after his.

We had many adventures together, and a boy couldn't have asked for a more loyal friend. I miss him to this day.

I'd always been taught that because dogs didn't have souls, they didn't go to Heaven when they died. They simply returned to the dust and ceased to exist, except within the memories of those who loved them.

I later became close to a much smaller dog. He was smaller only in terms of stature, and his name was Bo. He was a beautiful Long-Haired Dachshund who embodied the saying, "You're only as big as you think you are." Bo thought he was a Saint Bernard.

One of my fondest memories of Bo is an incident that happened while walking through a Georgia neighborhood on a fall afternoon.

Bo always walked with his head up. He was proud, but kind. As we walked through the neighborhood, he would often bark at much bigger dogs, as if to say, "I can take you!" Most of the other dogs didn't react at all to Bo, as they were big enough to shelter their egos from such a small physical specimen. That is until this particular day when Bo felt especially bold. We walked by a large dog that appeared to be a Doberman mix, and Bo started his noisy routine.

Two barks from Bo, and the dog leapt to his feet and charged us. Bo let out a high-pitched yelp and literally jumped up into my arms. The dog circled us several times, barking at Bo, who continued to bark right back from the safety of his perch atop my shoulders.

Finally the dog walked away. I set Bo down and he walked on as proud as he always did, except for the slight wobble in his knees.

A few years after that walk, Bo chased a wild duck into the street and was hit by a car.

How terribly depressing it would be for the story to end there, and for years, I thought it did. Yet as I began to study Heaven and the New Earth, I realized that those who taught me that animals were left out of Heaven were not only wrong in their concept of Heaven, but they were also making assumptions concerning who God wants around for eternity.

Quite simply, if God created animals to live forever in His ideal world (the Garden of Eden), why would God not have animals in the world He has taken back from Satan?

What good is a New Earth without animals? Not only that, but what about the fact that the Bible clearly tells us animals will be in Heaven?

A chariot pulled by horses took Elijah to Heaven (2 Kings 2:11). We are told there are many horses in Heaven because they are ridden by the vast armies of Heaven (Revelation 19:11, 2 Kings 6:17). Other animals probably aren't mentioned in Revelation because they don't play a role in the second coming of Jesus, but isn't it reasonable to believe that since there are numerous horses in Heaven that there are other animals too?

Isaiah 65:25 tells us that in Heaven:

"The wolf and the lamb will feed together and the lion will eat straw like the ox . . . They will neither harm nor destroy on all my holy mountain" (Isaiah 65:25).

According to God's description, not only will animals be on the New Earth, but they will apparently be vegetarians. I have difficulty imagining Bullet tearing into a big piece of broccoli, but I'm sure he'll have just as much fun as he did when we'd bring him leftover steak.

Also consider Romans 8:19-22:

"The creation waits in eager expectation for the sons of God to be revealed. For the creation was subjected to frustration, not by its own choice, but by the will of the one who subjected it, in hope that the creation itself will be liberated from its bondage to decay and brought into the glorious

freedom of the children of God. We know that the whole cre-
ation has been groaning as in the pains of childbirth right
up to the present time."

Notice that because the leader of the earth (Adam) fell, all creation fell along with him. Also note, *"the creation itself will be lib-*
erated from its bondage to decay and brought into the glorious free-
dom of the children of God."

God will restore all creation, not just man. It's *all* His, and the
devil had no right to take any of it. If animals were on the earth when
God had it all His way (Genesis 1:25), they will be there when God
chooses to have it that way again. If He is going to put humans back
on the New Earth, why *wouldn't* he place animals there as well?

DO ANIMALS
HAVE SOULS?

Whether or not animals have souls is irrelevant to them going to
Heaven. God could easily recreate animals on the New Earth with
or without souls.

However, for the sake of our study consider the following passage:

"[T]he Lord God formed the man from the dust of the
ground and breathed into his nostrils the breath of life, and
the man became a living being" (Genesis 2:7).

The King James Version translates *living being* as *living soul*, and man wasn't a "living soul" until God "breathed into his nostrils the breath of life." The Hebrew word is *nephesh*, and the Bible seems to say that God breathed it into animals as well in Genesis 1:30:

> *"And to all the beasts of the earth and all the birds of the air and all the creatures that move on the ground—every-thing that has the breath of life in it—I give every green plant for food."*

You see, when God breathed *nephesh* into Adam, Adam became *nephesh*. According to the Bible, God also breathed *nephesh* into the animals. Other passages that use this word concerning animals are Genesis 6:17; 7:15.

I'm not suggesting that animals have human souls, but I am suggesting that they have some kind of a soul—an animal one.

A COVENANT
WITH ANIMALS?

If you're still not convinced that God cares for animals and sees them as an important part of earth, consider the story of the Great Flood. Noah was to take representatives of all kinds of animals with him so that they wouldn't die out.

Perhaps the most interesting part of this story is that God made the post-flood covenant not only with man, but with the animals as well.

"Then God said to Noah and to his sons with him: "I now establish my covenant with you and your descendants after you and with every living creature that was with you—the birds, the livestock and all the wild animals, all those that came out of the ark with you—every living creature on earth" (Genesis 9:8-10).

Not only did God go into a covenant with animals, but when He purified the earth with the flood, and, in a sense, renewed it, God's plan for earth *still* included animals.

Just as God thought they belonged on the renewed earth then, I believe He will have them on the eternal New Earth of the future.

A large part of our duty as humans is to take care of and rule over earth's animals. God told humans to *"rule over the fish of the sea and the birds of the air and over every living creature that moves on the ground"* (Genesis 1:28).

We are also reminded that though we care for and rule over the animals, they ultimately belong to God:

"[F]or every animal of the forest is mine, and the cattle on a thousand hills. I know every bird in the mountains, and the creatures of the field are mine" (Psalm 50:10-11).

Ruling over animals means a variety of things. In Genesis 9 God tells Noah:

"The fear and dread of you will fall upon all the beasts of the earth and all the birds of the air, upon every creature that moves along the ground, and upon all the fish of the sea; they are given into your hands. Everything that lives and moves will be food for you."

Though at times most humans use certain animals for food, it seems that God has instilled within us a sense of responsibility for them in addition to His command to do so in Genesis 1:28.

Proverbs 12:10 says, "The righteous care for the needs of their animals..." Even in our increasingly secular-minded world, we have laws against cruelty to animals. Somehow, we know that animals should not be mistreated and that we owe them some sort of defense against harm.

It's a complicated balance that will not exist on the New Earth because all death will be dead. As it appears was the case in the Garden of Eden, there will be no meat eaters on the New Earth. Therefore, we will not use animals as a source of food.

GOD MADE ANIMALS FOR OUR COMPANY

As most of us remember from the story of the Garden of the Garden of Eden, God actually sent the animals to remedy Adam's loneliness until He fashioned Eve to be his partner (Genesis 2:18-19). That seems to provide insight concerning our natural friendship with animals. It's why most people can't resist petting a dog on the head or throwing a ball to begin a game of fetch.

After all, animals were God's idea, and it would simply be irrational to assume they don't belong on the earth where God originally placed them.

Just as God made angels different from humans, He made humans different from animals. He designed all of His creatures to function and interact with each other in the beginning, and He will restore that fellowship on the New Earth.

I'm convinced death has not stolen our pets forever, just as it has not stolen our family members and friends who have passed away.

God's plan is to reunite all of His creation again on the New Earth.

Consider the words of Colossians 1:19-20:

"For God was pleased to have all his fullness dwell in him, and through him to reconcile to himself all things, whether things on earth or things in Heaven, by making peace through his blood, shed on the cross."

What makes humans different from animals is that God gave us the choice to accept or reject His fellowship. Because God created animals differently, they don't have that choice. It's not that they are being taken to Heaven against their will; it's that they were created as simpler creatures that don't have the capacity to consider an alternative to God's rule.

Though we are different from the animal kingdom, we share similarities with them, the most important of which is that God created us both. Because of that, we should be reasonable and considerate in our treatment and care of animals.

IS IT IMPORTANT
TO STUDY HEAVEN?

Though I don't have all the answers, I wanted to share with you the benefits of our studies in this book. I also want to encourage you to study these things for yourself. Study God's Word and make your own conclusions.

That Satan does not want us to be reunited with God and His creation is one of the main lessons to take from this study.

From day one of human existence, Satan has done everything in his power to convince people to be their own gods. He's not going to stop until everyone has made their decision concerning God and God locks him away for eternity.

That is why it is important for us to educate ourselves concerning God's plans for Heaven.

WE MUST CHANGE
OUR ATTITUDES

"Can you help my marriage?" She asked in a trembling voice.

Before I could answer, she calmly said, "I only have about a year to live. I just want some precious moments with my husband before I die."

She told me of how her husband reacted to the news of her illness with total denial.

"He's mean to me and complains when he takes me for my treatments. It seems my illness has become a tremendous burden in his life, and he resents me for it. All I have to look forward to now is Heaven."

The way she said it left me at a loss for words.

By the tone of her voice, I could tell that she felt the sad part of all this was that she actually *had* to look forward to Heaven. All the better options, like living here, had been taken from her.

I must admit, I've felt that way in the past, and I certainly don't want to be critical of people in such difficult situations, but I think Christians as a whole need to stop viewing Heaven as a consolation prize. As discussed in previous chapters, this life is important. While we should not seek death or dismiss ourselves from the responsibilities of this life, we must change our attitudes concerning Heaven.

I believe that many of our struggles in life are because of Satan's efforts to steal us away from God. He wants us to reject God, not only because Satan hates us, but because he hates God and wants to take His children away in order to hurt Him.

Some of the tools Satan uses are false information and lies. The Bible calls him the "father of liars" in John 8:44.

Revelation 13:6 tells us that Satan *"opened his mouth to blaspheme God, and to slander his name and his dwelling place and those who live in Heaven."*

Note that Satan slanders three things: God Himself, God's people, and God's "dwelling place."

If Satan can fool non-Christians into believing that the Bible teaches that Heaven consists of ghosts floating around in the clouds in a boring, secluded and impersonal abstraction, fewer people will want to consider how they can go there.

Furthermore, if Satan can convince Christians of those same lies and misconceptions concerning Heaven, he has a good chance of dampening their passion to lead people to God.

In past conversations with other Christians about the afterlife, I remember hearing people say, "The main thing is that no matter what Heaven will be like, it will be better than Hell."

Sadly, their main reason for accepting Jesus as their savior was not because they wanted to be with God forever but because they were terrified of Hell.

Please don't misunderstand; I believe that a good, healthy fear of Hell is a great motivator to encourage us to take our actions and dedication to God seriously. But I also believe that if we only choose Heaven as an alternative to Hell, we are selling God short and are dooming ourselves to a lackluster faith that won't inspire anyone around us to choose salvation.

After all, I can think of *lots* of things that are better than Hell that I wouldn't want to experience for eternity. Examples include root canals, paying taxes, having headaches, packing for moves and having car trouble. But I wouldn't look forward to any of those things.

When Christians begin teaching that God has, through the sacrifice of Jesus, bought back not only humans, but also the earth and all creation to restore it to perfect form, our fears of the afterlife will subside and we will be much better witnesses for Christ.

We've got to start by teaching that Heaven is far more than a consolation prize, but rather the true desire of our minds, bodies and spirits.

CAN WE KNOW THAT WE ARE GOING TO HEAVEN?

I remember having a terrible dream as a teenager.

The dream was so bad that I awoke screaming and lay awake in bed until daylight.

I had dreamed about judgment day, but not the one for which I'd hoped.

In the dream, I watched from my window as Jesus took people from their homes to be with Him. I waited for Him to come for me, but He did not.

He eventually disappeared in the distance. The earth became eerily silent and in the distance I could see someone else.

It wasn't Jesus returning for me.

As the monstrously gigantic figure grew closer, I could tell who it was.

Satan.

We made eye contact, and I ran to hide. Somehow I ended up face down on my bed, praying for God to come back and save me, when suddenly the walls of the house rumbled as though an earthquake was striking. I felt the house rising toward the sky and looked out the window to see smoke. I ran to the window and peered outside to see the face of Satan. Fire covered the ground like a river, and the flames wrapped around him. He held my house in the palm of his hand and with his other hand he reached into the window to capture me.

That's when I woke up with a scream.

I've been through tornados, car wrecks and surgeries, but those experiences cannot compare to the terror that paralyzed my body after that nightmare.

The dream revealed my heart at that time. I didn't know what would happen to me if I died because my relationship with God had been suffering.

A few months later, I listened to a sermon on salvation and the words were very refreshing. Especially the words of 1 John 5:13:

"I write these things to you who believe in the name of the Son of God so that you may know that you have eternal life."

John wrote these words so that we can know we have eternal life. Not so that we'll "have the best shot at it" or so that we'll "feel a little better about it," but so that we can *know* we are going to Heaven to be with God.

It's more important for your name to be written in the Book of Life than it is for you to know exactly what Heaven will be like. It's also important that you know you are going to be with God so that when you speak to others you will speak with confidence and experience.

I want to encourage you to stay the course. As the old hymn sings, "Heaven will surely be worth it all."

Jesus said, *"I am the way and the truth and the life. No one comes to the Father except through me"* (John 14:6).

In this day, it's popular to consider ourselves too enlightened to *really* believe such a narrow claim. We don't want to appear judgmental, and we don't want to be considered a bigot.

It's dangerous for us to base our beliefs on what is politically correct or simply popular at any given time.

If we truly believed there were lost people on the earth today who were going to go to Hell when they died instead of the land of the redeemed, then we would be bolder in our approach with people. We wouldn't wait around, thinking that they will eventually be won over because we didn't "push our religion" on them. We also wouldn't be so timid that we rationalize our lack of personal evangelism by saying that we would have more influence on people by waiting until they ask us.

Jesus certainly didn't wait to be asked. Many times, His comments brought people to ask questions, but He often volunteered information to those within His influence without waiting for questions.

It was often His boldness that brought crowds to Him to learn.

Likewise, we need to be bold and confident so that we can bring people to Heaven with us. I'm certainly not saying we be rude or annoying, but we undoubtedly need to share the message of salvation by our words and actions as we live on this earth. Our willingness to share (or not) will have eternal significance.

CONCLUSION

Heaven and Hell are two very real places and there is no neutral ground.

None of our accomplishments on this earth mean anything at all if we are not on God's side when the day of judgment comes. Death comes for us all unless Jesus returns during our lifetimes. No amount of vitamins, minerals, exercise or medicine can prevent it from eventually happening.

God offers to give us our lives back. It is only He preventing permanent death for humanity. He is willing to forgive and forget the fall of man and restore things to the way He intended in the beginning when everything was youthful and fresh.

How could we possibly refuse His offer?

Live this life so that you will be with Jesus in Heaven. Conduct yourself around your friends and family so that you can have precious moments, long conversations and great adventures with them in Heaven on the New Earth.

I hope to see you there!

INTRODUCTION

1. Joe writes, "I was terrified by the entire concept of Heaven." Have you ever felt that way?

    _____

    _____

    _____

    _____

    _____

2. Do you think Christians discuss the topic of Heaven enough, too much or just the right amount? Why do you think that?

    _____

    _____

    _____

    _____

    _____

3. What times or events in life cause you to look forward to Heaven?

    _____

    _____

    _____

    _____

    _____

Chapter 1
HEAVEN IS AN ACTUAL PLACE

1. John 14:2 tells us that Jesus left to prepare a place for us. What does this passage mean to you?

   _____

   _____

   _____

   _____

   _____

   _____

2. Lee writes, "We often think that Jesus humbled Himself by working as a carpenter while in His human body, but I cannot imagine a more appropriate job for the Creator of the earth and stars than carpentry." Do you agree with this statement? Why or why not?

   _____

   _____

   _____

   _____

   _____

   _____

3. Why do you think the Bible provides us with "previews" of Heaven?

   _____

   _____

   _____

   _____

Chapter 2
WHAT WILL WE BE IN HEAVEN?

1. What about humans make us different from angels? From animals? From God?

    _____

    _____

    _____

    _____

2. What three parts combine to make a complete human?

    _____

    _____

    _____

    _____

3. Why do you think Jesus wanted the disciples and future readers of the Bible to know that He was not a ghost? (See Luke 24:37-39)

    _____

    _____

    _____

    _____

4. What does the Bible mean when it calls Jesus the "first fruits" of those who have died (1 Corinthians 15:20)?

    _____

    _____

    _____

    _____

5. Why do you think Jesus retained the scars on His hands in His new body?

    _____

    _____

    _____

    _____

6. Do you feel comfort in the words of this book concerning the recognition of friends and family members in Heaven?

    _____

    _____

    _____

    _____

7. According to Revelation 21, why will our new bodies not experience old age or deterioration?

    _____

    _____

    _____

    _____

8. What is a general belief of Gnosticism as discussed in this chapter? Why do you think so many Christians unknowingly believe Gnostic teachings as some did in Paul's day?

    _____

    _____

    _____

    _____

    _____

Chapter 3
WHAT HAPPENS WHEN HUMANS DIE?

1. Do you struggle with the concept of death in the same way that Lee did?

    _____

    _____

    _____

    _____

    _____

2. Do you pray for God to comfort you about this fear? If yes, in what ways has God comforted you?

    _____

    _____

    _____

    _____

    _____

3. Have you ever experienced an event like the one that happened to Todd? If not, do you believe such events occur?

    _____

    _____

    _____

    _____

    _____

    _____

4. Do you feel encouraged to know that "a great cloud of witnesses"
    watch us run our Christian race? (Hebrews 12)

    _____

    _____

    _____

    _____

    _____

    _____

5. What does the Bible mean when it tells us to "set [our] minds on
    things above" but then tells us to take this life seriously as well? What
    are ways we can combine these two concepts?

    _____

    _____

    _____

    _____

    _____

    _____

Chapter 4
WHERE IS HEAVEN?

1. What are the three uses of the word "heaven" in the Bible?

_____

_____

_____

_____

_____

_____

_____

_____

_____

_____

2. Why should we be leery of anyone who claims to know the exact location of Heaven?

_____

_____

_____

_____

_____

_____

_____

_____

_____

_____

_____

Chapter 5
LIFE IN THE NEW WORLD

1. Lee tells a story about his dad teaching him to drive by first having him drive in an empty parking lot. He then says that God expects us to give proper focus to the little things in this life so that we can be trusted with larger responsibilities in this life and in Heaven. How do you think we can do this? What things in this life might prepare us for Heaven?

_____

_____

_____

_____

_____

2. In what ways is this life different from God's original intent?

_____

_____

_____

_____

3. In what ways do you struggle with the temptation to be your own god? What are you doing to put your trust in God and not in your own abilities and efforts?

_____

_____

_____

_____

_____

4. This chapter discusses loving "this world" while at the same time understanding that we are to separate ourselves from this world in its present form. How can we do this?

    _____

    _____

    _____

    _____

5. Before reading this chapter, did you imagine a Heaven with absolutely no work or tasks? If so, why did you imagine this and in what way, if any, has your view changed?

    _____

    _____

    _____

    _____

6. What do you think 1 Corinthians 6:2 means? What about 2 Timothy 2:12?

    _____

    _____

    _____

    _____

7. Why do you think it is not popular to discuss different rewards and responsibilities in Heaven?

    _____

    _____

    _____

    _____

Chapter 6
WILL THERE BE ANIMALS IN HEAVEN?

1. After reading this chapter, do you think animals will be in Heaven? Why or why not?

    _____

    _____

    _____

    _____

2. What do you think Romans 8:19-22 means?

    _____

    _____

    _____

3. In what ways did God establish a covenant with animals?

    _____

    _____

    _____

4. To whom do animals belong?

    _____

    _____

5. If you've lost a pet to death, how does this chapter make you feel?

    _____

    _____

    _____

    _____

Chapter 7
IS IT IMPORTANT TO STUDY HEAVEN?

1. Do you think it is important to study Heaven? Why or why not?

    _____

    _____

    _____

2. What three things does Revelation 13:6 tell us Satan blasphemes/slanders? Why does he do this?

    _____

    _____

    _____

3. Have you ever had a nightmare like the one Lee described in this chapter?

    _____

    _____

4. According to 1 John 5:13, why did John write his book?

    _____

    _____

5. In what ways can we teach our friends about God's gift of salvation and Heaven?

    _____

    _____

    _____

    _____